T0022203

A PET NAMED ANXIETY

A PET NAMED ANXIETY

Life with the World's Cutest Companion from Hell

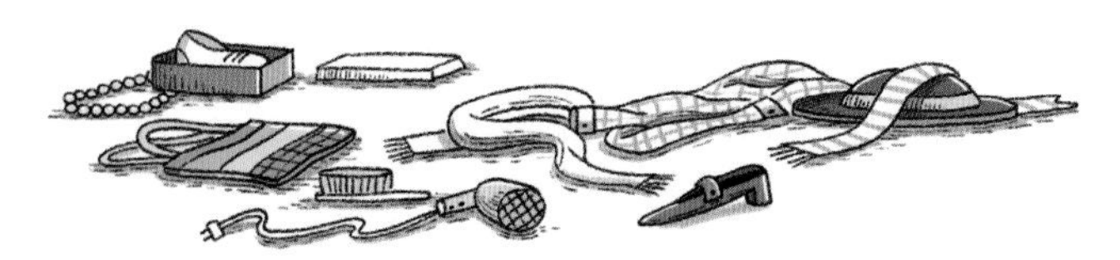

SYLVIE SWENNI illustrated by PAULA BOSSIO

CASTLE POINT BOOKS
NEW YORK

Printed in China.
For information, address St. Martin's Publishing Group,
120 Broadway, New York, NY 10271.

www.castlepointbooks.com

Castle Point books are published and distributed by St. Martin's Publishing Group.

ISBN 978-1-250-28529-4 (paper over board)
ISBN 978-1-250-28530-0 (ebook)

Illustrations by Paula Bossio
Design by Katie Jennings Campbell
Editorial by Monica Sweeney

First Edition: 2023

10 9 8 7 6 5 4 3 2 1

To an overthinking, furniture-rearranging,
nonsense-texting little pet.
—S. S.

To a chatty, impulsive, stubborn,
clingy, cowardly, and crazy pet: mine.
—P. B.

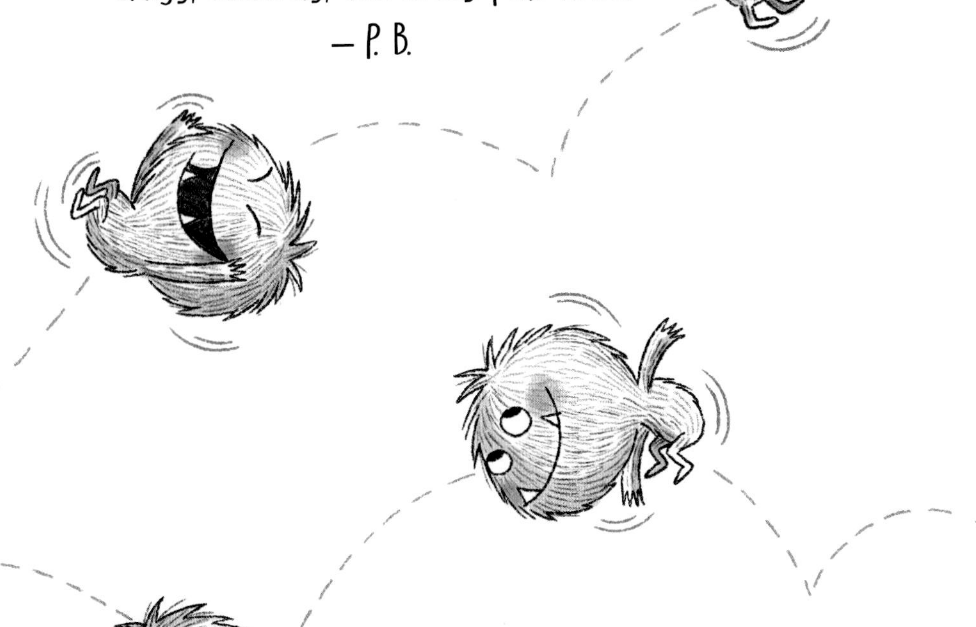

Meet my pet, Anxiety!

(My adorable little hellbeast!)

ANXIETY

It ran wild

again.

It does this when I'm nervous.

Or actually...

OVERWORKED
HUNGRY
ANTSY
SUCCESSFUL
HESITANT
TIRED
LOW
SAD
WORRIED
HAPPY
EXPECTANT
UNDERWHELMED
WORRIED
WIDE AWAKE
UNAPPRECIATED
AN IMPOSTER

It just happens
all the time.

Let me catch it before
it causes trouble.

BLACK
HOLE OF
EMOTIONS

Or leaps into the void.

You see,
my pet, Anxiety—
it hangs out in
the background.

BSHRR!

And yet it's always
in the way.

Let's take a walk,
so I can show you
what I mean.

Look, there it goes,
rummaging through my stuff.

What's mine is its,
and what's its is...

ugh, also mine.

Every morning,
it's up and at 'em.

It keeps me from
getting dressed.

It makes a mess
all over my house.

It helps itself to my food.

And runs up my
credit card bills.

SHOP
T.V
FRAG

It barks its
head off
at my sister

And should
probably
apologize.

BZZZ

WAIT.

Here we go again.

GREAT! FANTASTIC A BIT
NO WAY SORRY! YEAH! NO!
THANKS YES! FINE HAHAHA
I KNOW
READY NO!
PLEASE! HAHAHA
COME ON! OH MY GOD

But there's
no stopping it
now.

WOW, MARRY ME...

JUST KIDDING,

UNLESS YOU'RE NOT,
HAHA HAHA!

It's completely obsessed with my phone,

and sounds
like a psychopath.

6AM HIKE? TOOOTALLY!

But, wait,
this one's a doozy.

An event my Anxiety
cannot miss!

Yup, it followed me
on my date, that little...

son of a

It runs off its leash
and says all the
wrong things.

I'm dying alone,

at this rate.

My pet Anxiety
is not a quitter.

So it loves to
show up at work.

Its biggest strength
is staring blankly.

And its biggest
weakness?

It just cares too much.

It picks out my flaws
from thin air.

I'M JUST SAYING YOU SOUNDED UNPREPARED

I LOVE THIS SONG!
IM...SH VHHSHY... WE...SH
HIP!
I'M NEVER DRINKING AGAIN

And it will try anything.

But I've been learning
to train it from
the day it was born.

GRRRW!

I feed it positive thoughts.

I take it for
walks,
runs,
and hikes.

I give it belly rubs
and manicures.

And I taught it
to meditate.

I even got it into journaling so it could barf out all its thoughts.

Some days it seems like
it's hitting the road.

And on others it
just clings to my side.

Today might be the day
that everything is fine!

Nope, just kidding!

It's about to lose
its freaking mind.

I'll need to
give it time
to recover.

KEEP
OUT!

And be caring with myself.

We're both just
doing our best.

GO TEAM

It's my pet, Anxiety.

(My adorable little hellbeast!)

It has a life of its own.

But I can nurture it
as a piece of me,
and show it where to go.

And I know
I'm not alone.